SHADOWS
of the
KING

SHADOWS
of the
KING

Pastoral Meditations on the Book of First Kings

Clint Humfrey

Paul Toews

Terry Stauffer

Gavin Peacock

Jeff Jones

2015

Shadows of the King: Pastoral Meditations on the Book of First Kings

Copyright © 2015 by B. Clinton Humfrey, Paul H. Toews, Terry J. Stauffer, Gavin K. Peacock, and Jeffrey Jones.

Published by Calvary Grace Church of Calgary
204 6A Street NE
Calgary, Alberta T2E 4A5
www.calvarygrace.ca

All rights reserved. This book or any portion thereof may not be reproduced or used in any manner whatsoever without the express written permission of the author(s) except for the use of brief quotations in a book review or scholarly journal.

Cover design: Jamie Ballak

Cover photo: © Vencavolrab | Dreamstime Stock Photos & Stock Free Images

First Printing 2015

Trade paperback ISBN: 978-0-9949882-0-1
PDF ISBN: 978-0-9949882-3-2
Mobipocket ISBN: 978-0-9949882-2-5
ePub ISBN: 978-0-9949882-1-8

Unless otherwise indicated, all Scripture quotations are from the ESV® Bible (The Holy Bible, English Standard Version®), copyright © 2001 by Crossway, a publishing ministry of Good News Publishers. Used by permission. All rights reserved.

Scripture quotations marked (NLT) are taken from the *Holy Bible*, New Living Translation, copyright ©1996, 2004, 2007, 2013 by Tyndale House Foundation. Used by permission of Tyndale House Publishers, Inc., Carol Stream, Illinois 60188. All rights reserved.

Dedication

To the saints of Calvary Grace Church of Calgary, Alberta, Canada, our beloved flock, on the 19th of November 2015, the ninth birthday of our fellowship.

Acknowledgements

This collection of essays owes much to others besides the five of us. First, we all need to acknowledge the continuing support of our wives, Christel Humfrey, Melody Toews, Erin Jones, Juanita Stauffer, and Amanda Peacock, and of our children. Without their constant encouragement and prayer our ministry would not be possible.

Similarly, we also need to acknowledge the ongoing and prayerful support and encouragement we receive in our ministry from our congregation at Calvary Grace Church of Calgary. We are thankful to serve, in the words of the biblical writer, these saints "with joy and not with groaning" (Heb. 13:17).

Others have contributed materially to this project in particular, knowingly or unwittingly. Several in our congregation reviewed certain chapters and gave feedback, and we are grateful to them. Juanita Stauffer's grammatical review of the final manuscript is greatly appreciated. The cover art and design was the skillful work of Jamie Ballak. Daniel Melvill Jones was instrumental in creating EPUB and MOBI e-book formats of this book. Finally, we would be remiss if we did not mention the tireless administrative efforts of our church secretary, Gail Harfield, who made it much easier for us to make time in our schedules to work on this project.

Above all, we joyfully acknowledge the God and Father of our Lord Jesus Christ, without whom we are nothing and our works are worthless, and to whom belongs all glory and praise. Amen.

Contents

Preface xi
    Clint Humfrey

CHAPTER 1: The Origin of the Book of Kings 1
    Jeff Jones

CHAPTER 2: *Pax Solomonica*: Solomon's Golden Age as a
    Hinge of History 11
    Clint Humfrey

CHAPTER 3: David's Succession: Lessons for Fathers 19
    Gavin Peacock

CHAPTER 4: Wisdom in the Godly Life 25
    Paul Toews

CHAPTER 5: The Fall of Solomon: A Case Study 31
    Gavin Peacock

CHAPTER 6: The Pathway to Idolatry in First Kings 37
    Jeff Jones

CHAPTER 7: The Doctrine of God in the Elijah Narrative 45
    Terry Stauffer

APPENDIX A: Chronologies of Rulers, Prophets, and
    Events in the Book of Kings 53
    Jeff Jones

APPENDIX B: Further Reading 61

Index 65
About the Authors 69
About Calvary Grace Church 71

Preface

Clint Humfrey

"You live on dead dreams. You live on the myths of the past. The glory of Solomon is gone! Do you think it will return? Joshua will not rise again to save you nor David! There is only one reality in the world today! Look to the west, Judah! Don't be a fool, look to Rome!"

Messala to Judah Ben-Hur in *Ben-Hur (1959 film)*.

Long ago, at many times and in many ways, God spoke to our fathers by the prophets, but in these last days he has spoken to us by his Son, whom he appointed the heir of all things, through whom also he created the world.

Hebrews 1:1-2

When New Mexico Governor Lew Wallace wrote the epic story *Ben-Hur* he was writing more than what is today called "historical fiction." Wallace, whom history remembers as the man who offered amnesty to Billy the Kid, was a careful student of first-century history. Wallace used the Jewish resistance to Roman occupation in Judea as the backdrop to what he called "*A Tale of the Christ*." *Ben-Hur* expresses the tension of longing for past prosperity and hoping against hope for a secure future.

No tension would exist for the Jewish Diaspora if it were not for the climactic achievement of Israel's united monarchy under David and Solomon. Those were the golden years. Since 1948, the resurgent hopes of ethnic Jews have been brought together under a common flag bearing the symbol of the Star of David, the national flag of the nation-state of Israel. Tensions from both past and future remain in the lives of Israelis to this day and the legacy of David and Solomon lives on.

But the achievement of David and Solomon, like all powerful stories, and all true history, has a tragic thread. The warrior David could not consolidate the theocracy by building a temple. God would not allow it. The sage Solomon failed as well. He took up the task of completing the temple only to have it stripped and burned by successive conquerors.

What went wrong? How could the geo-political climax of the Old Testament turn into the first step towards national exile? The book of First Kings offers us the answer. Written from the perspective of the sad end, it traces the glory of Solomon, while hinting at the sources of corruption that would bring his downfall. As with all tragedy, the root cause is the sin within. Sin was and is the problem—which is why First Kings remains relevant as a living text, a witness from the Holy Scriptures, and a narrative for souls that are "prone to wander, Lord, I feel it, prone to leave the God I love," as the hymnwriter put it.

In the Christian church, First Kings is one of the sections of the Bible that is often neglected. That is why I suggested that the pastors of Calvary Grace Church in Calgary, Canada, the church I serve as lead pastor, should preach through the main sections of First Kings in the fall of 2015. Alongside our study for our sermons, we wrote a series of essays that have been compiled into this edited volume. The intention of the essays is to show the abiding relevance of the Holy Scriptures, and the ways in which even lesser known Old Testament texts are in fact part of "a tale of the Christ." Luke records how Jesus Christ, as he walked on the road to Emmaus, could span the entire Old Testament and elucidate "the things concerning himself." To follow the example of Jesus has been the aim of the authors of this volume, both in discipleship and in method.

While intended to be a simple collection of essays, it should be observed that the work required to write them, arrange them, and edit

Preface

them is hardly simple. The authors are all pastors of Calvary Grace Church, so the essays bear the marks of regular ministry among the flock of God. These men are distinguished by Gospel-centred piety combined with the shepherd's ability to lead sheep to healthy food. I wish to thank Pastors Paul Toews, Terry Stauffer, Jeff Jones, and Gavin Peacock, who added essay writing to their regular preaching demands in order to fulfill my whims for "a side project." Special thanks are due to Pastor Jeff Jones who edited the essays for publication in his usual gracious, yet militarily precise, manner!

My prayer to God is that readers of this volume will see that God has not failed in keeping his promise, to David, of a Son who would sit upon his throne forever. In the Gospel, Jesus Christ, God incarnate, took on flesh and dwelled among humankind, in order to be a mediator between God and humanity, even through his own sin-bearing work on the cross, being the substitute for his people, the objects of his love. And it is this Jesus who died, rose again on the third day, was attested by many witnesses, and ascended into heaven. Those who believe in this Messiah recognize that he is not only the Son of David, but is the Son of God, and is coming again to judge the living and the dead. All readers are gladly summoned to heed this King, who calls them to turn and follow him, now and forevermore. Amen.

CHAPTER 1

The Origin of the Book of Kings

Jeff Jones

Authorship

As with many other books of Scripture, the authorship of the single work we divide into First and Second Kings has been a contentious matter of debate in scholarly circles. Paul House observes that the various theories can basically be divided into two groups—single-author theories and multiple-author theories.[1] He concludes that the single-author option is best for several reasons, including the evident unity of the book (and its unity with Joshua, Judges, and Samuel—see below), the use of a wide variety of material in keeping with ancient standards of historiography, and the fact that it permits reliance on the text itself rather than the often-mutually-exclusive speculative reconstructions common among multiple-author theories.[2] In other words, single authorship is the simplest explanation and adequately explains the text.

The author of First Kings is anonymous. There are no indications in the letter or elsewhere in Scripture who might have written the book. Jewish tradition ascribes the book to the prophet Jeremiah, largely due to connections between Jeremiah 52 and Second Kings 24-25, but this seems unlikely.[3] As the book seems to have been written during the exile

---

[1] Paul House, *1, 2 Kings*, New American Commentary (Nashville: Broadman & Holman, 1995), p. 29.

[2] Ibid., pp. 38-39.

[3] Gary Inrig, *I & II Kings*, Holman Old Testament Commentary (Nashville: Broadman & Holman, 2003), p. 2 (Kindle edition: location 279).

1

in Babylon (see below) and since Second Kings' final chapter's report on Jehoiachin's elevation from disgrace by Babylon's king indicates an understanding of events in Babylon, the author was probably resident in Babylon with most of the Jewish exiles. Since Jeremiah never went to Babylon, this makes him a far less likely candidate to have written the book.

For the Christian reader, this means that Kings should be read as the work of one divinely inspired hand. The reader needs to expect unity, consistency, and an overall flow in reading the text and remember that the human author had a specific audience in mind and his own particular points he wanted to make. On the other hand, Christians should be wary of speculation about the precise identity of the human author used by the Holy Spirit to write the work.

Unity with Joshua, Judges, and Samuel

The book of Kings continues a theological history of Israel in the Promised Land begun in the book of Joshua and which continues through Judges, Samuel, and ends in Kings. Indeed, First Kings "picks up" where Second Samuel "leaves off." The seamless nature of this "handoff" echoes similar "handoffs" between Deuteronomy and Joshua (Moses' death), Joshua and Judges (Joshua's death), and Judges and First Samuel (Samuel's role as a unifying final judge).[4] As House argues, "Using many ancient sources this author composed Joshua-Kings as a sweeping account of Israel's tragic loss of the land it was promised in the Pentateuch."[5]

While we cannot be certain, of course, House's suggestion seems to be one of the best explanations for the book. If that is indeed the case, then First Kings cannot be fully understood outside of the context of the books that came before it. The Christian reading First Kings today,

---

[4] House, p. 38.
[5] Ibid., p. 39.

CHAPTER 1: The Origin of the Book of Kings

then, will benefit most by reading through Joshua, Judges, and Samuel first, and ensuring they read Second Kings afterward.

Place of Origin

As already noted, Kings appears to have been written from Babylon, during the exile. The story comes to an end with the gracious elevation of Judah's king Jehoiachin by Babylon's king Evil-Merodach in the thirty-seventh year of his exile (2 Ki. 25:27-30). The precise nature of the report indicates either access to an official record of the event, a record that by its nature would have been a Babylonian court document, or having witnessed this elevation personally. Either option argues for a Babylonian location for the author of Kings.

Another indication of a Babylonian provenance for the book of Kings is the literary role of the Jehoiachin elevation. Given the author's repeated stress throughout Kings on God's promise to David (1 Ki. 2:24; 8:15, 20; 9:5; 2 Ki. 8:19), the theological intent of this section seems to be to give hope to Israel's exiles, by showing that David's line endures despite God's judgment on Israel and that therefore God has not forgotten his promises. If the author were writing after the exile, surely he would have noted the return from exile as a further illustration of God's faithfulness (as, for instance, the author of Chronicles does in Second Chronicles 36:22-23 by recording the edict of Cyrus).

Further support for a Babylonian origin is the variety and nature of the sources the author uses. He employs various annals and chronicles from both Judah and the northern kingdom of Israel, weaving them into a seamless account. Where did he get access to all these documents? Probably the best explanation, I humbly suggest, is that he found them in Babylon's libraries. Such documents—annals, court records, chronicles, treaties, etc.—would have been a treasure trove of diplomatic and military intelligence to any invading power. Surely Babylon was keenly interested in any documentation they might find about Jerusalem's diplomatic relationships with Babylon's current and potential rivals (say, for instance, the Egyptians). Therefore, I believe it quite likely that the Babylonians would have been careful to carry away as many Jewish records as they could find before firing Jerusalem.

I find this explanation attractive not only because this explains how a Jew in Babylon could have access to Judah's court records, but even more because it also explains how he could have obtained access to the records of the northern kingdom of Israel—a nation destroyed almost two hundred years before he wrote. Since Babylon had, similarly, conquered Assyria, the nation that destroyed Israel's capital Samaria in 722 BC, I think it likely that the Babylonians had "inherited" from Assyria's own archives the records that the Assyrians had presumably, and for similar reasons, taken from their defeated peoples. If this is true, a Jewish author exiled to Babylon would have, in the remarkable providence of God, been in an ideal position to research and write an account of Israel's history.

One of the key differences between Kings and Chronicles, then, is perspective—the first being an *exilic* work and the second a *post-exilic* work. The Christian reader, when reading the two works, will gain much by keeping this distinction, and thus the two distinct original audiences of the two works, in mind.

Sources

Accepting a single author for Kings, or even calling him an "author" in the first place, does not ignore the fact that he used many sources in composing the book. Our anonymous author was a historian of the first rate, as his careful use and repeated citations of source material makes clear. The text of 1 Kings records explicit references to three sources: the Book of the Acts of Solomon (1 Ki. 11:41); the Book of the Chronicles of the Kings of Judah (1 Ki. 14:29; 15:7, 23; 22:45; cf. 2 Ki 2:23); and the Book of the Chronicles of the Kings of Israel (1 Ki. 14:19; 15:31; 16:5, 14, 20, 27; cf. 2 Ki. 1:18 and many other references). The Christian reader must not confuse the references to the latter two works

CHAPTER 1: The Origin of the Book of Kings

with the canonical books of Chronicles, which were written after Kings and could not have been used as sources.

Moreover, the phrase "to this day" is used several times in First Kings. Interestingly, in at least two cases, this reference describes a state of affairs that, actually, could not be the case any longer when the author of Kings wrote his book: first, the poles of the Ark being visible outside the Holy of Holies "to this day" (1 Ki. 8:8); second, the reference to certain peoples being drafted as slaves of the Israelites "to this day" (1 Ki. 9:21). Far from disproving the veracity and inerrancy of Scripture, these references actually uphold them. They indicate that the author of Kings is faithfully representing the actual content of his source material, content that clearly had been written at a time when those facts were still true, and so they stand as evidence for the historical accuracy and detail of Kings.

The use of sources should not at all be understood to mean that the author of Kings was a mere plagiarist, simply repeating what he read elsewhere. The text makes plain that Kings is a carefully curated collection of historical events, a selection drawn from these sources for the author's purposes. In more than one place the author notes that various historical details, presumably irrelevant for Kings' literary and theological purposes, have been left out and the reader may consult his source directly for that information. For example, the author makes reference to the fact that the details of Zimri's conspiracy (1 Ki. 16:20) and the "might that [Omri] showed" (1 Ki. 16:27) may be found in the Chronicles of the Kings of Israel, as can the details of Ahab's city-building and ivory palace (1 Ki. 22:39).

The Christian reader, then, needs to understand that while Kings was written to make a theological point, it is no less a historical work for it. Indeed, the historical accuracy of the facts reported in Kings is critical to the integrity of the case that Kings' author is making. The care with which the author researched this history makes plain that he viewed the importance of historical accuracy in this way.

Date of Writing

The final exile to Babylon took place in 587 or 586 BC. However, the reader must understand that this was not the only deportation, but was actually the last of three events in late Judahite history where the Babylonians sent large numbers of Hebrews to Babylon. The first took place in 605 BC during the reign of Jehoiakim, and was the deportation where Daniel and his friends were sent to Babylon (Dan. 1:1-4). The second took place in 597 BC, and involved the removal and deportation of King Jehoiachin (2 Ki. 24:10-17) as well as the prophet Ezekiel (Ezekiel 1:2 seems to mark the date in reference to this exile).

The last date recorded in the book of Kings is the elevation of Jehoiachin, described as occurring in the twelfth month "in the thirty-seventh year of [his] exile" (2 Ki. 25:27). The twelfth month of the thirty-seventh year after 597 BC would put his elevation somewhere around 560 BC, providing the earliest possible date for the completion of Kings. The edict of Cyrus in 538 BC serves as the latest possible date for the book's completion as such an event would most likely have been noted in the text. However, Persia conquered Babylon the previous year, an event that might have given the Jews hope of a return, and since this event is also unrecorded in Kings it seems that the book would have been finished before that date.

The most likely range of dates, then, for the completion of Kings would be the period between 560 and 539 BC.

Genre

Kings has features of several literary genres. It is, first of all, a narrative. It tells a story. Events unfold in a roughly chronological order (though the author does step backward and forward several times as he moves between the accounts of the Israelite and Judahite kings). There is a clear plot to the book,[6] as the story begins with the heights of

CHAPTER 1: The Origin of the Book of Kings

Solomon's glory, moves through the crisis of the northern kingdom's secession, and recounts the ups and downs and victories and losses of the various kings. It has a climax (followed by an editorial commentary) in the destruction of Samaria in Second Kings 17, followed by the heights of Hezekiah's reforms, and the crisis of the Assyrian invasion. The low point of the book is the reign of Manasseh, which is followed by another "height" in Josiah's reign, perhaps the most faithful king recorded in the book. His sudden and untimely death makes clear that the plot is still moving toward tragedy, and the book does, indeed, climax again and finally in the destruction of Jerusalem. Nevertheless, the author leaves the reader with a note of hope, with the story of Jehoiachin's elevation and restoration of some of his dignity—a foreshadowing of the promised restoration of Davidic rule.

There is characterization in Kings as well.[7] Solomon is a tragic figure, given every advantage and failing in the end, and his story is echoed and contrasted in some ominous ways by Jeroboam, another tragic figure. There are villains—ruthless, evil figures like Jezebel, Athaliah, and Manasseh, and rather hapless but still wicked men like Ahab. There are flawed heroes like Elijah and Hezekiah. There are earnest men like Josiah and the prophets whose faithfulness and fleeting success made no earthly difference in the end.

Kings is not only narrative, however. It is no mere myth or fairy tale or fictional thriller. Kings is clearly a historical work as well, given its attention to historical detail and meticulous referencing of source material. However, like other historical works in the Bible, it is not "mere" history. The author's selective use of source material has already been pointed out, and so this anonymous author clearly had an objective or point in mind as he sifted through and selected historical events to record.

The author's objective in Kings is inescapably theological. While some critics will assume that a theological agenda undermines the

---

[6] For a more detailed examination, see House, pp. 61-64.
[7] Again, House has a good discussion of characterization in pp. 64-67.

historicity of the book, this simply is not the case. First, it must be pointed out that every author has an agenda, not merely religious authors. Second, an author with a theological agenda, particularly an agenda that aims to uphold the Law of Moses—which includes harsh prohibitions of false witness!—should in charity be assumed to be writing in keeping with his stated beliefs. Third, as already pointed out, the author is using historical events to make theological points about God's faithfulness to his promise, in contrast with and despite the faithlessness of his people; an author with an agenda to underline God's faithfulness would only be undermining his own objective if he had no care for historical truth.

Finally, Kings provides the fullest historical and theological development, up to its time of writing, of a concept stemming from Deuteronomy 18: the raising of a "prophet like Moses." Certainly prophets appear prior to Kings in the Joshua-Kings narrative, but it is in Kings where prophetic activity "explodes." Kings, and especially its Elijah/Elisha account, describes the full flowering of the role of God-inspired prophets holding kings, nations, and people accountable to the covenants God has made with them.

Paul House argues for such reasons that probably the best description of the genre of Kings would be "prophetic narrative."[8] My only reservation about such a description would be that a "prophetic narrative," in principle, need not be historically accurate; one could have a moving and inspiring fictional prophetic narrative, for instance. I would therefore, humbly, suggest a slight modification to that genre identification might be to emphasize the vital importance of historical truth, and so call Kings an example of *"prophetic-historical narrative."*

For the Christian reader, then, Kings is to be read as a narrative, paying attention to plot and characterization and other narrative elements. It is to be read as history, understanding that these were real people involved in real events, and that they connect with our "real world" precisely because of their historical accuracy. Finally, it is to be

---

[8] Ibid., p. 57.

CHAPTER 1: The Origin of the Book of Kings

read as a prophetic work, much like a sermon, actually—an account that reviews the shape of God's work in history, with the objective of calling God's covenant people to trust in him and to faithful living for his glory.

CHAPTER 2

Pax Solomonica: Solomon's Golden Age As A Hinge of History

Clint Humfrey

Introduction

"As for me, I have set my King on Zion, my holy hill."

Psalm 2:6

"Uneasy lies the head that wears a crown..."

Henry IV, Part 2 by William Shakespeare (Act III, Scene I).

When an empire is on the rise it often leads to what has come to be known as a golden age. Such a time is often an age of peace (Latin: *pax*) which has been hard-won by war. Throughout history there have been several such eras, like the *Pax Romana* of the early Empire, or the *Pax Britannica* of 19th century Victorian England, or the *Pax Americana* of the Post-World War II era.[9] All of these eras of peace were established by

---

[9] For Christian reflection on human empires, see Augustine, "City of God," in *Nicene and Post-Nicene Fathers*, Series 1, Volume 2, Philip Schaff, ed.). On the state of the *Pax Americana* from an economic perspective, see Dambisa Moyo, *How the West Was Lost: Fifty Years of Economic Folly and the Stark Choices Ahead* (Vancouver: Douglas & McIntyre, 2011). For a contemporary Christian response to the waning of the *Pax Americana*, see Os Guinness, *Renaissance: The Power of the Gospel However Dark the Times* (Downers Grove: Intervarsity Press, 2014).

ruling empires. But as with all nations and kingdoms, they rise and they fall.

So it is even with the people of Israel. The Patriarchs were given promises that carried the people through slavery in Egypt all the way to the Promised Land and the establishment of a settled nation. But even Israel, as it ascended from judges to kings, would not be able to maintain the *Pax Solomonica*, Solomon's international peace. The golden age under David and Solomon was also the beginning of a gilded age, a time when things looked shiny on the outside but the inside was decaying. Israel divided into north and south, and the golden age was over, even as the Egyptian Pharaoh carried away the golden shields from the temple and Rehoboam was left to replace them with mere bronze (1 Ki. 14:27).

Up From Slavery and Jealous of Giants

Before the time of the golden age, few would have expected Israel, a nation of former slaves that had suffered frequent setbacks, to become an established people at peace. The Philistines with their champions like Goliath of Gath were effective in limiting any permanent gains made by Israel's various judges.[10]

Israel became distressed at the lack of permanency they had, and so they wanted more than periodic judges. They wanted a king just like the surrounding nations (1 Sam. 8:20). Though it was a declaration of their unbelief, God permitted the request, and temporarily upheld Saul to rule Israel. Though Saul looked like a Jewish giant,[11] he was weak in faith and jealous by nature. God would reject Saul for his disobedience and anoint an unlikely shepherd boy as the next king of Israel, overlooking other more eminent and giant-like candidates.[12]

---

[10] Cf. the example of Gideon's clandestine threshing of wheat in the winepress (Judg. 6:11), or Saul's army at Goliath's taunt: "they were dismayed and greatly afraid" (1 Sam. 17:11).

[11] "...head and shoulders taller than anyone else in the land" (1 Sam. 9:2, NLT).

[12] See God's response to Samuel at the rejection of David's tall brother Eliab: "Do not look on his appearance or on the height of his stature, because I have rejected

CHAPTER 2: *Pax Solomonica*

During Saul's Philistine campaign, the stalemate between the two armies illustrated the old problem: neither people was strong enough to completely conquer the other. Absent in Israel was faith in the Covenant LORD who had split seas and filled them with slaughter. Yet the anointed boy, fresh from his flocks, came to the battlefield and was affronted by the blasphemy of it all. David said:

> What shall be done for the man who kills this Philistine and takes away the reproach from Israel? For who is this uncircumcised Philistine, that he should defy the armies of the living God? (1 Sam. 17:26)

Goliath's subsequent defeat was not so much a testimony to David's slinging skill, but to the ability of Yahweh to deliver his people in an Exodus-like way. David's subsequent military conquests as a courtier of Saul should have encouraged a modest response along the lines of John the Baptist ("He must increase, but I must decrease," Jn. 3:30) but instead Saul grew more jealous.

Songs of Zion

Even as an outlaw, David was able to respect the office which Saul held as God's king while growing in a personal faith in the Covenant LORD. David's "Cave of Adullam" piety (1 Sam. 22) was expressed in ageless poetry and resonant song. As Saul turned from dark moods to darker magic (1 Sam. 28) David was being prepared for life as the ruler and defender of God's people. When Saul and Jonathan were slain in battle (2 Sam. 1:25), David was rightly grieved, but was also prepared to unify the tribes of Israel, eventually establishing Jerusalem as the new centre of God's people. In this way, God *chose* Zion to be the pinnacle to which the nations would be summoned to look.[13] Zion would not be

---

him. For the Lord sees not as man sees: man looks on the outward appearance, but the Lord looks on the heart" (1 Sam. 16:7).

merely a symbol of earthly power, but of the establishment of God's rule and reign on the earth through his chosen regent (Ps. 2).

Pax Davidica

Zion, the former Jebusite stronghold conquered by David (2 Sam. 5:6-10), was missing something. It needed the special presence of Yahweh. So David brought the Ark to Jerusalem, in a foolishly trivial way at first but then with great deliberation and joyful demonstration (2 Sam. 6). The worshipful procession of the Ark to Jerusalem was the inauguration of the very highest point in Israel's history (2 Sam. 6:12-15).[14] It is no wonder that Israel under David could be described as having peace all around and rest from their enemies (2 Sam. 7:1). The *Pax Davidica* was established.

All that remained for David to do was to build a temple for the Ark. But that was where a great shift occurred. God did not permit David to house the Ark. Like Moses seeing the Promised Land from Pisgah, but being prohibited from entering in (Deut. 34), David had to look on in faith at what God intended to do. Though Solomon, David's son, would build a physical temple building to house the Ark, God was saying much more when he made the promise to David in Second Samuel 7:13 where God spoke of the Son of David: "He shall build a house for my name, and I will establish the throne of his kingdom forever."

A Hinge of History

There is no debate that the single greatest hinge of history is the life, death and resurrection of Jesus Christ. All of time has subsequently been understood as being either *before Christ* (BC) or *Anno Domini*, the "year of our Lord" (AD). This is the hinge upon which all history must have

---

[13] See Ps. 132:13; 78:68

[14] Cf. the processional language of Psalm 24, as the Ark enters Jerusalem.

CHAPTER 2: *Pax Solomonica*

reference.

But prior to the advent of Christ, the transfer of the monarchy in Israel—God's chosen people—is a very important hinge. From David, the man after God's own heart, to Solomon, the wise one, there turns on these two hinge-pins the rise and fall of Israel's kingdom.[15]

We see the overlap of good and bad in the transition from David to Solomon. The rise and decline are in tension as we see David, who is renowned for piety, involved in first an adulterous affair with Bathsheba and then a subsequent intrigue to murder her husband (2 Sam. 11). David and Bathsheba's union would produce the immediate successor to David's royal throne in their son Solomon (2 Sam. 12:24).

Solomon as a young man was declared the heir, despite both his controversial parentage and a succession crisis with Adonijah (1 Ki. 1). In this transfer of power, Solomon showed practical savvy that would be expected from a king. He consolidated his power so that the narrator of Kings could say that "the kingdom was established in the hand of Solomon" (1 Ki. 2:46). But native smarts were not all that Solomon had. He piously requested from Israel's God the gift of wisdom. God was pleased with this request (1 Ki. 3:10), which showed the continuity between David and Solomon. The heir gladdened the heart of God as the father had. David had been given unprecedented military victories beginning with the defeat of the Nephilim-like Goliath. So too, had Solomon been given what was unprecedented—an insight into the created order of the universe that made his court a magnet for scattered Gentiles in search of guidance and meaning (1 Ki. 4:34). The prosperity of Israel under Solomon would seem to flow naturally from the reign of a divinely endowed philosopher-king.[16]

---

[15] What I am calling a 'hinge' is essentially the schema put forth by Graeme Goldsworthy which divides Old Testament history into Part I (Genesis 1 to 1 Kings 10) and Part II (1 Kings 11-Malachi). See *Christ-Centered Biblical Theology: Hermeneutical Foundations and Principles* (Downers Grove: Intervarsity Press, 2012), p. 26.

[16] Cf. how the idealized philosopher-kings were described much later by the Greek philosopher Plato, circa 380 BC, in his work *The Republic*, 5.473d.

Pax Solomonica

Because of David's bloody victories, Solomon ruled a domain so secure that it sounds to the modern ear like a description of middle-class suburbia with "every man under his vine and under his fig tree, all the days of Solomon" (1 Ki. 4:25). This was the *Pax Solomonica*, "Solomon's Peace." There was inordinate wealth, international prestige, and domestic ease (1 Ki. 10). No greater symbol of the extensive peace of Israel was exhibited than the temple. Built with extravagant materials and employing the great luxuries of time and manpower in its construction, the temple was a spectacle by design (1 Ki. 6). Here was "Solomon's Peace" given full expression. The temple was a place where Israel was noticeably *settled*. They could worship in peace. They could live in peace. Their Promised Land was a portal to heaven. What more did they need?

Of course the *Pax Solomonica* was not heaven on earth, and Solomon was not the Son of David whom God intended. That Son would have to come later. And the corroding, gilded externals of this supposedly golden age began to show in the same things that appeared to be symbols of blessing. Through treaties with Yahweh-denying nations (1 Ki. 3:1) and intermarriage with Yahweh-denying wives,[17] it is no surprise that Solomon and the people would turn from trust in Yahweh to denial of him (1 Ki. 11:3). The accumulation of military power (horses), financial power (gold), and dynastic power (wives) was in direct violation of Yahweh's commands for kings (Deut. 17). The historical pivot in this climactic hinge sees the once prayerful Solomon, as Yahweh's king, turning to the dark worship of demons, even promoting the "abomination of the Ammonites" (1 Ki. 11:7). We could say along with David, "How are the mighty fallen", (2 Sam. 1:25), but in the case of Solomon, unlike Saul and Jonathan, his fall has not come in battle. Solomon's problem is that he did not battle enough. His wives and the

---

[17] "Now King Solomon loved many foreign women, along with the daughter of Pharaoh: Moabite, Ammonite, Edomite, Sidonian, and Hittite women" (1 Ki. 11:1).

gods they worshipped drew Solomon's heart away from God, signalling the downward spiral of Israel's national history that remained even until the advent of Jesus, the Son of David.

A House For My Name

What the *Pax Solomonica* teaches us is that God intended to do more than merely establish a highly successful competitor to the best that human civilization had to offer. God didn't need to set up a rival to Pharaoh, Alexander, Caesar, Napoleon or Hitler. God was doing something entirely greater. The moral failures of the first human king, Adam (Gen. 3), were replayed in the life of every human being and every subsequent ruler. Solomon was no exception.

The decline of God-honouring kingship with Solomon[18] saw the rise of God-commissioned messengers. In the fall of the monarchy was the rise of prophecy. As Israel and Judah receded into an ebb and flow of apostasy and renewal, the kings took on a secondary role. During the divided monarchy, during the exiles to Assyria and Babylon, and finally during the return to Jerusalem, the prophets took centre stage. Consider how massive a portion of the Old Testament records the words of these God-ordained prophets.[19]

What was the message of these prophets? They spoke of a new king who was to come. The new king would be the Son of David, but would be greater than Solomon. The new king would be wise, not merely as another Solomon, but one who embodied wisdom for the people. The new king would draw all the nations to himself, in a way that would make the Queen of Sheba's trip to Solomon seem insignificant. The king would see the nations coming to him, in order to *worship him.*

The prophets' predictions would be fulfilled with the advent of the "anointed one," the *Meshiach* (Hebrew) and *Christos* (Greek), Jesus, the

---

[18] Goldsworthy observes, "Solomon's being all but ignored in the New Testament" due to his colossal apostasy (p. 127).

[19] See the helpful chart in Goldsworthy, p. 26; cf. p. 163.

Son of David. This king would bring something better than the prosperous peace of Solomon, for he said of himself, "something greater than Solomon is here" (Matt. 12:42, Luke 11:31). He offered something more than a *Pax Solomonica*. He brings the *Pax Christi*, the peace of Christ, so that even rebels like Saul of Tarsus could be brought not only to submit to this king but to exhort all other rebels, saying, "let the peace of Christ rule in your hearts" (Col. 3:15). Only in Jesus Christ can the name of God reside in a person's heart. That is why only the Son of David could build for God "a house for my name":

> The one who conquers, I will make him a pillar in the temple of my God. Never shall he go out of it, and I will write on him the name of my God, and the name of the city of my God, the new Jerusalem, which comes down from my God out of heaven, and my own new name (Rev. 3:12).

CHAPTER 3

David's Succession: Lessons for Fathers

Gavin Peacock

Introduction

First Kings begins, "Now King David was old and advanced in years. And although they covered him with clothes, he could not get warm" (1 Ki. 1:1). David was waning and one of his sons, Adonijah, in collusion with Joab, David's army commander, planned to take over the throne. David eventually took action and made Solomon king, but it took Bathsheba to remind her husband that Solomon was the heir according to David's promise.

Solomon succeeded David to the throne. However, in the story of David's succession we see the results of both wise and foolish fatherhood. In other words, David's inconsistencies as a father were vividly displayed in the way he dealt with his sons, and in the consequences for his life, for their lives, and for the kingdom of Israel.

So what lessons can fathers learn from David?

Fathers Must Discipline Their Children

David's regular failure to discipline his children is highlighted in First Kings 1:6. Speaking with reference to Adonijah, the author says:

His father had never at any time displeased him by asking, 'Why have you done thus and so?' He was also a very handsome man, and he was born next after Absalom.

David indulged Adonijah. He sinned by omission in not correcting him and training him. The result was a spoiled and disobedient son who eventually turned into an entitled young man. But this was not the first time David had failed in this regard. You only need to look back in Second Samuel 13 to see David neglect his responsibility to execute justice when his son, Amnon, raped his half-sister Tamar. Amnon was lustful, devious, immature, and violent. An undisciplined child had grown into an evil man. The further result of David's abdication of the discipline of Amnon was that his other son, Absalom, became hardened and embittered against his father's lack of justice. Seeking revenge, he eventually killed his own brother, Amnon, and fled from his father (2 Sam. 13:23-29).

David knew he had not taken decisive action with Amnon, but realized that if he forgave Absalom he would be admitting his error. Nevertheless, he dithered again and did not ban Absalom completely. Then, when Absalom eventually returned to the king's presence, nothing was resolved: "…he came to the king and bowed himself on his face to the ground before the king, and the king kissed Absalom" (2 Sam. 14:33). David did not deal with Absalom's heart, so his son's bitterness remained. It eventually led to Absalom's death. Like Eli before him (1 Sam. 3), David knew about the evil of his children yet consistently neglected to restrain and correct them.

Fathers must discipline their children (Eph. 6:4). Acting early prevents ruinous consequences later because a child left undisciplined today will become the bane of society tomorrow. When he exercises justice, a father shows care for the child he disciplines, and (if it is the case), for the one his child sins against. However, too often fathers are afraid to "displease" their children: they are afraid of pushback, or a bad reaction. Especially with teenagers there is often a fear that they will run

CHAPTER 3: David's Succession

away or indulge further in sin if a father imposes correction and restrictions. Ultimately a father who doesn't discipline is seeking his own comfort. In that case, the father has forgotten his responsibility as head of the home and as the primary authority over his children. Too often the authority structure is reversed.

Solomon says in the book of Proverbs, "Folly is bound up in the heart of a child, but the rod of discipline drives it far from him" (Prov. 22:15). Discipline does not always require corporal punishment, like spanking, but it always involves training and correction. Fathers who will not exercise biblically mandated authority sin by their omission, doing harm to their children and others through them.

Nevertheless, fathers must discipline with the right attitude—not being harsh or domineering, so as to provoke children to anger (Eph. 6:4). In other words, the impatient self-serving attitudes and actions of a severe father can cause a child to become disheartened. But indulgent, negligent fathers who don't discipline biblically may actually provoke their children to anger and resentment through their lack of loving correction, as in the case of Absalom.

Finally, fathers must discipline their children by dealing with the heart issue behind their sin. They should angle their children towards what pleases the Lord, not simply their father. They must display the displeasure and the mercy of God in their discipline, always pointing their child towards the grace of the cross of Christ. Behavior modification is superficial. So much of a father's work is heart work. Remember, Amnon, Absalom, and Adonijah had rebellious hearts that were never dealt with.

So we can see that David's consistent, sinful failure to discipline his children had widespread reverberations, resulting even in the deaths of three of his sons. Even when we are saved in Christ, our sin always has consequences.

Fathers Must Be Examples To Their Children

It is ironic that Amnon's, Absalom's, and Adonijah's sins reflect David's sins of commission. David was greedy, sexually immoral, and murderous, committing adultery with Bathsheba and having her husband Uriah killed (2 Sam. 11). The immediate consequences were seen in the death of David and Bathsheba's child (2 Sam. 12). David was not a good example to his children.

Fathers must *be* what they teach their children. Otherwise, a child will see a hypocrite. They will follow what they see in their father's life as much as what they hear from their father's mouth. There should be no gap between a father's life and doctrine. Integrity of character is king because a father must not only teach his children what to do, but he must show them how it's done.

A father can be a bad example to his children if he speaks to and treats their mother harshly. Sons may think that is the way to treat women, and daughters may think that is the way they should expect to be treated. The sins of the father are then repeated in the children.

Fathers Must Teach Their Children

For all David's failures to discipline his sons and to be an example to them, he is not without merit. He was still a man after God's own heart (1 Sam. 13:14; Acts 13:22). He did teach Solomon. Solomon's Proverbs, which are written in the early chapters as a father's instruction to his son, indicate that David taught him the fear of the Lord as a child (Prov. 4:3-4).

1. Fathers should teach their children from an early age.

David taught Solomon from a "tender" age (Prov. 4:3). There is a time when the spirit of a child is most flexible and that is when they are

CHAPTER 3: David's Succession

young. Character building in the early years is far easier than later on when bad habits are ingrained.

2. Fathers should teach their children to love and obey God.

David says to Solomon:

> …be strong, and show yourself a man, and keep the charge of the LORD your God, walking in his ways and keeping his statutes, his commandments, his rules, and his testimonies, as it is written in the Law of Moses, that you may prosper in all that you do and wherever you turn (1 Ki. 2:2-3).

A father's instruction must always be in the context of commitment to God's ways and words. David tells his son, "be strong," and shows that true strength is connected to obeying God. In the New Testament Paul tells fathers, "…bring them up in the discipline and instruction of the Lord" (Eph. 6:4). He has Christian teaching in view.

3. Fathers should teach their children biblical masculinity and femininity.

David also passes on some final words of instruction to Solomon as he passes on his throne to him. David's instruction to Solomon is distinctly masculine. He says, "show yourself a man" (1 Ki. 2:2). That means there is particular manly behavior, which is different from that of a woman.

David unpacks this as leadership involving sacrificial provision and protection for the sons of Barzillai, and exacting justice upon Joab and Shimei (1 Ki. 2:5-9). He teaches Solomon what it means to be a man. Fathers must not only teach their children to love God and obey him. They must also teach them to be a biblical man or woman, not simply a generic Christian.

The Son of David Redeems Fatherhood

In many ways David is like many fathers today. He was, in fact, a mixed bag as a king and as a father, even in his kingly role of governing and nurturing his own children. His faults show how the sins of those in leadership can impact others, and consequently demonstrate the responsibility of those fathers who lead their homes. David's sins of commission as well as omission had devastating effects in his life, the lives of his children and in the lives of those around. And Solomon's successes were learned in the hard school of failures with Amnon, Absalom, and Adonijah. But God never intended to make David our ultimate example. His failures showed the need for a perfect King and a perfect Father.

God promised that this King would be from David's line and would rule in righteousness reflecting the perfect, loving rule of his Heavenly Father (2 Sam. 7:12-15; cf. Jer. 23:5). The true Son of David, Jesus Christ, redeemed David's fatherhood and all fatherhood, and through his atoning death and resurrection, he alone leads us to our one true Father in heaven (John 14:6-7). Now, in the New Covenant, Christian fathers are able to reflect God's fatherhood and Christ's kingly rule towards their own children.

CHAPTER 4

Wisdom in the Godly Life

Paul Toews

Introduction

In reading the wisdom literature of the Bible, one is confronted with three words that are seemingly used interchangeably: knowledge, understanding and wisdom. In fact, in order to understand wisdom, it is important to know how these words relate to each other and the differences between them. Having a clear picture of what wisdom entails, we can then discern the central role wisdom plays in living a godly life. Though highly significant in godly living, wisdom is not enough. It needs to be fuelled by obedience.

The Nature of Wisdom

In our world there are a great many things that we can know. These pieces of information form our knowledge base. The more we know, the more we have to work with, but this doesn't mean we understand. Just as students may know their times tables, it doesn't mean that they understand the concept of multiplication.

A collection of facts and bits of information, or knowledge, doesn't guarantee understanding but is essential to understanding. Note that when the Lord gave Solomon wisdom and understanding, he also gave him breadth of mind like the sand on the seashore (1 Ki. 4:29). This was especially evident in his knowledge of the natural world. If understanding is thought of as seeing the big picture or how discrete bits of information relate to each other, then it makes sense that understanding is richer if it has more to work with. Once a person understands, true learning has occurred and is evident in being able to apply knowledge to new situations. Solomon was able to apply what he knew of nature, even human nature, to life and skillful living as seen in his many proverbs and sayings. He was also able to take what he knew about a mother's love for her child and apply it when making a decision in the case of the two prostitutes (1 Ki. 3:16-28).

This is the heart of wisdom. It is knowing what to do and when to do it. It is the "so what" of learning. It is seen primarily in the decisions we make as we go about life. Hiram of Tyre was hired by Solomon to help build the temple as he was "full of wisdom, understanding, and skill for making any work in bronze" (1 Ki. 7:13-14). He knew about bronze. He knew its characteristics and how it could be worked. He knew the temperatures at which it needed to be heated. He knew what tools were available. He understood how these facts related to one another, and then, in wisdom, was able to make decisions about how best to use it in the building of the temple.

Living, like metalwork, is very much a skill. In order to live well one must learn how to live skillfully. We constantly take what we know and understand of the world, nature, and people, and apply it when we decide how to act in new situations. We filter through our knowledge and decide what to do and when to do it. So, everyone, Christians and non-Christians alike, live with wisdom. The term applies to both and yet the quality of wisdom between the two is as different as day and night.

Wisdom and Godliness

James 3:13-18 distinguishes between wisdom that comes from above and wisdom that is earthly. Jealousy and selfish ambition results in an application of knowledge—in wisdom—that results in disorder and every vile practice. He calls it earthly, unspiritual, and demonic. This

CHAPTER 4: Wisdom in the Godly Life

stands in stark contrast to wisdom that comes from above, that leads to a harvest of righteousness or which can be described as a godly wisdom.

Realizing now that there is an earthly wisdom and a godly wisdom, how do we assess our wisdom as a follower of Christ? Tom Schreiner says that wisdom means living under God's sovereign rule in the particulars of everyday life.[20] How do wisdom and godliness relate?

To answer this question we need to first understand what godliness is. I really like Thomas Watson's definition. He says, "Godliness consists in an exact harmony between holy principles and practices."[21] It is application of what we know about God and spiritual truths to the way we live. Wisdom is godly in that our practices, the things we do or the way we are, flow out of and reflect an understanding of spiritual truth and principle.

The fear of God is both the beginning of wisdom (Ps. 111:10, Prov. 9:10) and is itself wisdom (Job 28:28). This fear of God is not a servile fear. Rather, it is like a child who respects and loves his parents and wants so much to please them. He is not afraid of punishment as much as he is afraid of displeasing one who is the source of love and security.[22] Similarly, fear of God for the Christian is a desire to please our Father who is our source of love and security. While God will never stop being our source of security and love we rightfully fear anything that may threaten its flow. We fear that which would offend and displease the one we love. Not only is this the beginning of wisdom, leading to further displays of wisdom, it is in itself a wise disposition to cultivate.

---

[20] Thomas Schreiner, *The King In His Beauty: A Biblical Theology of the Old and New Testaments* (Grand Rapids, MI: Baker Academic, 2013), p. 286.

[21] Thomas Watson, *The Godly Man's Picture* (Carlisle, PA: Banner of Truth Trust, 1992), p. 7.

[22] R.C. Sproul, (2014, August 1). "What does it mean to fear God?" (blog post). http://www.ligonier.org/blog/what-does-it-mean-fear-god/ Retrieved August 28, 2015

Wisdom and the Godly Person

What does this mean for the godly person? If we desire this wisdom, what are we to do? First, the knowledge and understanding we gain must be ours. We are the ones who live our lives. We need to know what to do and how to be in different situations. This knowledge has to be constructed and appropriated ourselves. If we want to know what pleases our Father, we need to be students of his Word. We need to gain knowledge of the things that please God. We don't have an app by which we can instantaneously access our pastor's knowledge in these matters as we go about our daily life.

Secondly, understanding is largely socially mediated. This means that we need each other. It is true that the Lord opens the eyes of the blind and grants us understanding (Acts 26:18). He does this through his Word (Rom. 10:17). This means we need to have the authors of the Bible talk to us through the Word, but we also need to be connected to a body of believers. We need to hear good preaching and teaching. We need to read good books by others who share their understandings. We need to discuss spiritual things with our brothers and sisters. As spiritual "facts" are discussed and deliberated upon, we gain understanding.

Third, it is accessible to all, but we need to desire and pray for it. Wisdom, personified in Proverbs, cries out to be heard in the street and markets (Prov. 1:20-33). It is available to all who would find it. It keeps us upright in a crooked generation and keeps us from stumbling in our walk through life (Prov. 4:11-12). By it we discern the way we should go and the things we should do (Prov. 14:8). It is described as precious and to be desired above all else (Prov. 8:10-11). It is a gift of God and so we have to pray (Jas. 1:5-6, 17). God delighted to grant wisdom to Solomon. He delights to grant wisdom to us. We desperately need it.

Finally, it should be noted that wisdom is not enough in leading the godly life. Knowing what to do doesn't mean we have the will to do it (Rom. 7:1-6). Consider Solomon who surely knew the command given to Israel's kings not to acquire many wives lest his heart turn away (Deut. 17:17), and yet he took for himself many foreign women who turned his heart from being devoted to the Lord (1 Ki. 11:1-8). He knew what was right but didn't do it. When we pray for wisdom, let us be sure to pray for the will to follow in its path.

Conclusion

Solomon was given wisdom to rule his people, which is essential if a king is going to rule his people in righteousness and justice (cf. Ps. 72). Surely Israel, at last, had its promised king, the one who would usher Israel into its intended glory! Yet he wasn't that king. He was merely a pointer. Solomon failed to remain faithful to the Lord. Not only would the king Israel needed have to be wise, but he would have to be perfect in his obedience. Praise be to God, we know this king who is greater than Solomon—Jesus Christ (Matt. 12:42). Not only is he wisdom incarnate (Col. 2:3, Isa. 33:5-6), he is without sin. His wisdom is coupled with a perfect desire to do what is right and the perfect will to carry it out. He is our King. He is our wisdom, the very wisdom of God (1 Cor. 1:24). Will you listen to wisdom? Will you follow?

CHAPTER 5

The Fall of Solomon: A Case Study

Gavin Peacock

Introduction

Spiritual decline begins with the small things. Unwise, but seemingly innocuous, choices can lead to full-blown folly. There is a downward spiral of sin and we can read of it from the wisdom of David in the gateway to the book of Psalms: "Blessed is the man who walks not in the counsel of the wicked, nor stands in the way of sinners, nor sits in the seat of scoffers" (Ps. 1:1).

First you walk, then you stand, then you sit in sin. To put it another way, first you tolerate sin, then you rationalize sin, and then you identify with sin. We should also remember that sin always has consequences, and this is more widespread in the case of a leader. First Kings 11 shows Solomon as a tragic case in point. He who started well finished badly. However, if the wisest of men can fall, no one is bulletproof.

Solomon's Disobedience

Wives, wealth, and false worship

At the peak of his power and the apex of Israel's religious and political prosperity, which comes to a climax in chapter 10, it is astonishing to read that Solomon's heart was turned away from God by his foreign wives (1 Ki. 11:1-4). This was in direct disobedience to Moses' law for marriage, which prohibited Israelites from marrying those from outside the covenant people of Israel because God had said "they would turn away your sons from following me, to serve other gods" (Deut. 7:4; cf. Ex. 34:15-16).

He also began to greedily accumulate excess wealth, whether that was gold and silver (1 Ki. 10:14-21, 27) or thousands of horses from his trade with Egypt (1 Ki. 10:26, 28-29). Excess money and wives also contravened Moses' instructions for kings:

> Only he must not acquire many horses for himself or cause the people to return to Egypt in order to acquire many horses, since the LORD has said to you, 'You shall never return that way again.' And he shall not acquire many wives for himself, lest his heart turn away, nor shall he acquire for himself excessive silver and gold. (Deut. 17:16-17)

The increasingly bad influence of his wives eventually turned his heart after other gods (1 Ki. 11:5), such that Solomon built altars of worship to Chemosh and Molech (1 Ki. 11:7-8). His disobedience and spiritual compromise led to full-blown idolatry and false worship. Solomon's lust for power through women and wealth meant that disobedience to God had become his "practice" (1 Ki. 11:11). He exchanged living in the fear of the Lord and obedience to his Word for worldly wisdom, and thought to protect himself through political strategy and monetary strength. He exchanged wisdom for folly and piety for pragmatism. This resulted in the wisest and most blessed of men breaking the primary command: "You shall have no other gods before me" (Ex. 20:3).

CHAPTER 5: The Fall of Solomon

Lost love, lost Word

Solomon's fall from grace began with an issue of the heart. He who loved the Lord now loved his foreign wives more, and the wealth, the political alliances, and the gods they brought with them (1 Ki. 11:2). "[H]is wives turned away his heart" (1 Ki. 11:3). His *heart* was not wholly true to the Lord like his father (1 Ki. 11:4) and the Lord was eventually angry with him because his *heart* turned away from him (1 Ki. 11: 9). Solomon lost his first love.

Solomon lost his first love and he also lost God's Word. First Kings 11:10 says God twice appeared to him "and had commanded him concerning this thing, that he should not go after other gods. But he did not keep what the Lord commanded" (cf. 1 Ki. 11:11). Solomon failed to heed God's warnings and God's Word. In this he also disobeyed Moses' instructions to kings, who were to write out the Law of Moses, read it, and obey it (Deut. 17:18-20).

Divine Consequences and Divine Sovereignty

Divine consequences

We read in First Kings 11:9 that "the LORD was angry with Solomon, because his heart was turned away from the Lord, the God of Israel, who had appeared to him twice...." Then God says to Solomon, "I will surely tear the kingdom from you" (1 Ki. 11:11).

Solomon's disobedience leads to divine consequences. Note that God promises to tear the kingdom from his hand, and so he raises up enemies to execute this judgment (1 Ki. 11:14-40). God often removes his protection from those who persist in disobedience and uses human means to accomplish his judgments.

Solomon's rise and fall also shows how the promises in Genesis 12:1-9 of land, rest, and worship were enjoyed and thrown away. Israel had conquered Canaan, built a temple, and enjoyed material and relational peace with other nations. Yet Solomon's, and Israel's, spiritual decline led to division and eventually exile. When Solomon lost love for God, he lost thankfulness to God. Unthankful people don't value God's grace to them, and, like Eve in the Garden, become wise in their own eyes and look for satisfaction in other things (cf. Gen. 3:1-7). As with Adam and Eve, the divine consequence is division and alienation.

The consequence of Solomon's idolatry was also national idolatry, which shows that leadership sins have devastating effects. The temptations to wealth and power are even stronger for those in authority, but we are all susceptible, and all sin has ripple effects in the community. This means no one can afford to coast. Solomon's example illustrates the need to remain obedient to God alone in a pluralistic, multicultural, and secular age. Standing firm on the rock of Scripture, on faith in Christ as the only way of salvation, and on the implications of Christian ethics will be a great challenge in the days ahead. True success as a Christian is measured by faithfulness and obedience to God.

Divine sovereignty

Yet God sovereignly designs Solomon's tragic failure as a pivotal point in redemptive history that propels us into the prophetic era (Ahijah, Elijah, Elisha and Isaiah in First and Second Kings; then Jeremiah, Ezekiel and the Twelve Minor Prophets). The prophets speak God's Word for God, calling back a disobedient people, and pointing them forward to the promised Son of David (2 Sam. 7:12-15; cf. Isa. 11:1-9). The kings fail to be obedient and Israel fails to be obedient, so the need for a true King and a true Israel is all the more evident.

God is not caught off-guard by these failures. The promise made to David was never going to be fulfilled in Solomon (2 Sam. 7:13-15). God is faithful where his chosen people and even the best of his leaders are not. He sovereignly judges Israel, even raising up enemies to punish Solomon, but mercifully remains true to his own promise to David. The Lord judges for the Lord's purposes. And these themes of judgment and mercy continue through the Old Testament until they collide on the cross. Christ fulfills the promise of a King with an everlasting kingdom, who will live in the fear of the Lord, and who will bring a righteous and peaceful rule (2 Sam. 7:13-15; cf. Isa. 11:1- 9).

Conclusion

Though Solomon's reign ends tragically, the Chronicler still points to him as an example of a good reign (2 Chr. 11:17). However we can see hints of the beginning of disobedience, which led to these tragic consequences, even further back. We read in chapter 3 that "Solomon loved the Lord, walking in the statutes of David his father, *only he sacrificed and made offerings at the high places*" (1 Ki. 3:3, emphasis added). Even though he may be excused because there was no temple at this point, he still perhaps shows a tendency to compromise. The point is that spiritual declension begins with small things in unusual places. For all Solomon's wealth and wisdom, he forgot that it was from God and for God.

Let us take heed lest we fall. Let us be watchful of our own sinful tendencies and Satan's temptations to turn our hearts from God. And let us keep our hearts right by cultivating love for God in Christ through meditation upon, and obedience to, his Word. One greater than Solomon has come. Jesus Christ is our wisdom (Matt. 12:42; 1 Cor. 1:30).

CHAPTER 6

The Pathway to Idolatry in First Kings

Jeff Jones

Introduction

The book of Kings is in one sense the story of *two* kings, and of the lines that followed them. On the one hand, Kings presents the glorious yet imperfect example of wise Solomon, and the kings descended from him. On the other hand, beginning with the division of Israel under Solomon's son, Kings follows the northern king Jeroboam and those who succeeded him. There is a clear comparison and contrast between these two lines right from the beginning.

Solomon's key role in First Kings is establishing God's temple (chs. 5-9:9). Jeroboam, too, is pictured as establishing temples and indeed an entire system of worship with altars and images and priests and a calendar (1 Ki. 12:25-33). Jeroboam, like Solomon's father David, is repeatedly described by Kings in comparison with monarchs who succeeded him (1 Ki. 16:2, 7, 19, 26, 31; 22:52; 2 Ki. 3:3; 10:29, 31; 13:2, 6, 11; 14:24; 15:9, 18, 24, 28). And both kings fell to doctrinal compromise—Solomon in allowing high places, and Jeroboam by going a step further and erecting golden calves and a non-Levitical priesthood—thus establishing a pattern of idolatry that neither of their royal lines escaped, and which ultimately resulted in their ruin.

The High Places

Solomon's failure is made plain almost at the beginning of his account, in the author's summary judgment on Solomon's reign: "Solomon loved the Lord, walking in the statutes of David his father, *only he sacrificed and made offerings at the high places*" (1 Ki. 3:3).[23] Many people of the Ancient Near East understood mountaintops as "sacred spaces" where deities lived and could be encountered.[24] A high place could have an open-air site, an altar, a pillar or pole, or even a temple.[25] In the book of Kings, the high places represent such a serious problem that toleration of high places is the primary "measuring stick" by which the author assesses the monarchs who followed Solomon.

Solomon establishes a wicked pattern. Under his son Rehoboam, Judah "did what was evil....*For they also built for themselves high places*" (14:22-23). Asa and Jehoshaphat did "what was right" in God's eyes but *"the high places were not taken away"* (15:11, 14; 22:43). The second half of Kings continues the theme as Jehoash, Amaziah, Azariah (Uzziah), and Jotham all "did what was right in the eyes of the Lord" but the "high places were not removed" (2 Ki. 12:2-3; 14:3-4; 15:3-4, 34-35). Briefly Hezekiah interrupted this pattern: "And he did what was right in the eyes of the Lord, according to all that David his father had done. *He removed the high places....*" (2 Ki. 18:3-4). But Hezekiah's son Manasseh *"rebuilt the high places* that Hezekiah his father had destroyed" (2 Ki. 21:3). The narrator so despises these alternate places of worship that he devotes almost a whole chapter to a blow-by-blow description of Josiah's campaign against the high places (2 Ki. 23:5-20).

---

[23] Emphasis added here and in all Scripture quotations in this chapter.
[24] Victor Matthews, *Manners and Customs of the Bible* (Peabody: Hendrickson, 2006), p. 41.
[25] Paul House, *1, 2 Kings*, New American Commentary (Nashville: Broadman & Holman, 1995), p. 75.

CHAPTER 6: The Pathway to Idolatry in First Kings

Rejection of God's Place

It's easy to think of high places as locations for pagan worship, and they were. Yet First Kings indicates that Yahweh was worshiped at these places as well: "The people were sacrificing at the high places, however, *because no house had yet been built for the name of the Lord*" (1 Ki. 3:2). Indeed, prior to the temple's construction, First Kings reports that Solomon worshiped God at "the great high place" of Gibeon: "And the king went to Gibeon to sacrifice there, for that was the great high place. Solomon used to offer a thousand burnt offerings on that altar" (1 Ki. 3:4). Therefore, the construction of the temple was, among other things, intended to end such worship: "You shall surely destroy all the places where the nations whom you shall dispossess served their gods, on the high mountains and on the hills and under every green tree.... *You shall not worship the Lord your God in that way*. But you shall seek the place that the Lord your God will choose out of all your tribes to put his name and make his habitation there. There you shall go...." (Deut. 12:2, 4-5).

Note carefully, then, that God here specifically outlaws *worship of himself* at these high places (Deut. 12:4). Idolatry was not the only important issue with the high places. Their existence after the temple's dedication represented a blatant rejection of Jerusalem,[26] and thus a refusal to worship God in the way he has ordained.

A Competing Worship System

Solomon's spiritual compromise was rooted in disbelief. God promised that if Solomon served him with a whole heart, Solomon's royal line would last forever (1 Ki. 9:4). Yet Solomon chose to guard his kingdom not through wholehearted obedience but through diplomacy, marrying numerous foreign princesses (1 Ki. 11:1-3) and tolerating high places to keep them happy (11:8). Jeroboam, similarly, was promised a

---

[26] Ibid.

"sure house" if he followed God wholeheartedly (11:38). Just like Solomon, he failed to trust God and sought security by political means. Fearful of losing his people's loyalty as they traveled to Jerusalem's temple, he established a rival worship system at home (1 Ki. 12:26-27). Both kings wanted God's blessings, but refused to follow God's appointed way to receive those blessings.

Jeroboam's choice of golden calves was carefully considered, as he "*took counsel* and made two calves of gold" (12:28). He consciously echoed the golden calf of Sinai, for his language is almost identical to Exodus 32:4 ("these are/behold your gods, O Israel, who brought you up out of the land of Egypt!"). In Exodus, Aaron, who in the very next verse declares a feast "to the LORD" (Yahweh), seems to have intended an alternate means of worship rather than an alternate deity. In Kings, similarly, given Jeroboam's naming of his son Abijah ("Yahweh is my father"), and given the pagan habit of portraying their gods as standing or seated on bulls or calves, Jeroboam is probably presenting these calves as "platforms for Yahweh" rather than replacements of him.

"Everyone Doing Whatever is Right in his Own Eyes"

Jeroboam may well have rationalized his changes as serving Yahweh, but nevertheless they violated Scripture. Exodus 32 already made clear God's disapproval of Aaron's similar actions. Similarly, Jeroboam's replacement of Jerusalem ("you have gone up to Jerusalem long enough" [1 Ki. 12:28b]) sought to avoid God's appointed place of worship, just as the temples he built on high places violated Deuteronomy 12 and his appointment of non-Levitical priests violated Deuteronomy 18:5.

God alone gets to define how he is worshiped. Jeroboam and Israel wanted to do things their own way. However, that simply isn't how one worships God, as the prohibition of high places makes clear. Deuteronomy 12 tells Israel that they are *not* to simply worship God any way they pleased: "You shall not do according to all that we are doing here today, *everyone doing whatever is right in his own eyes...*" (Deut. 12:8). That phrase, first used in Deuteronomy to describe a stiff-necked people in the wilderness, and then ominously repeated in the book of Judges, sums up the fundamental heart attitude that ultimately led to Israel's destruction at the end of Second Kings.

Applications

1. There is only one place to find God.

Centralized worship is a vital theme of First Kings. God appoints the place where people will come to him, not man. God appointed Jerusalem, Mount Zion, as that place, and his glory filled the temple Solomon built as a sign that he would receive Israel's worship there.

In the New Covenant, God has, once again, appointed only one place, Jesus Christ, where worship may be offered and salvation may be found. Jesus himself, immediately after upholding the Old Testament principle of centralized worship, told a Samaritan woman that soon worship would be offered not in Jerusalem but "in spirit and truth" (John 4:20-24)—meaning he who is "the truth" (John 14:23), the one who sends the Holy Spirit (John 15:26), is the one whose body is the true temple destroyed and rebuilt in three days (John 2:19-21). Jesus himself said that "no one comes to the Father except by me" (John 14:6). While our world would dearly love to be able to find salvation at other "high places" such as Buddhism or Islam or Hinduism, God has never tolerated a "many ways, many places" approach to worship, and he does not tolerate it now.

2. There is only one way to worship God.

In the New Covenant there remains such a thing as "acceptable worship" (Heb. 12:28) and so, by implication, there is "unacceptable worship." Acceptable worship approaches God with reverence and awe (Heb. 12:28). On the other hand, Christians do not relate to God merely as terrified subjects, but are adopted as sons (Gal. 4:5). Christians can therefore approach God just as Jesus does, as a loving father, calling him "Abba" (Rom. 8:15; Gal. 4:6).

Christians struggle with this balance. On the one hand, David Wells has lamented that "God rests only lightly upon the church."[27] The spirit of ancient Israel, which uncritically assumed Yahweh's blessing upon pagan practices in his worship, such as high places and images, is alive and well in modern evangelical churches that happily import unbiblical practices like Eastern meditation, labyrinths, interpretive dance, and female pastors. On the other hand, some theological conservatives, like the Pharisees of Jesus' day, have shown a tendency to overreact against such liberal excesses by, for example, mandating equally unbiblical prohibitions of musical accompaniment, of hymns of human composition, of particular instruments, and of certain musical styles.

God defines how he is to be worshiped, not man, and has done so sufficiently and finally in his Word. This means that Christians need to observe the practices laid out in Scripture—preaching, baptism and the Lord's Supper, reading of Scripture, prayer, songs, hymns, and spiritual songs, and regular gathering together on the Lord's Day—and refrain from adding practices not mentioned in his Word. On the other hand, we also need to take careful note of how Jesus and Paul condemned those who sought to legislate in areas God chose not to define. Especially when compared to the painstakingly prescribed detail found in the worship commanded in the Old Covenant, the New Testament very conspicuously refrains to specify the length of worship services or sermons, the frequency of the Lord's Supper, musical style, the physical layout of the worship meeting, and other matters. Christians, then, in all things, are to be careful not to go beyond what is written—either to add forms of worship not prescribed, or to prohibit interpretations of those forms that Scripture leaves open.

---

[27] David Wells, *God In The Wasteland* (Grand Rapids: Eerdman's, 1994), p. 224.

CHAPTER 6: The Pathway to Idolatry in First Kings

3. Our relationship to God is God's, not ours.

Israel's fundamental problem in the book of Kings is that *"everyone* [was] *doing whatever is right in his own eyes."* Our culture loves that message, too. Every time we hear a person claim that they refrain from "organized religion" because "faith is something personal," this attitude reigns. Every time a wandering believer resists counsel and correction from other believers and persists in their ways, this attitude reigns. Every time a person rejects the teaching of Scripture in some contested area like the perfection of Scripture or gender roles or human sexuality or divine creation, this attitude reigns.

Again, the New Testament tells us: "You are not your own. You were bought at a price." If this applies to our bodies and our souls, it certainly applies to everything we do with those bodies and souls—and *especially* to our relationship with God. If we belong to Jesus, we don't get to pick and choose what we believe; we heed his words to "observe everything I have commanded you." We don't get to opt out of the gathered church; we belong to other believers and they belong to us. Most importantly, God is in charge, not us. Our thinking, our beliefs, our priorities are all to be arranged in relation to him. We conform to him. He does not conform to us.

CHAPTER 7

The Doctrine of God in the Elijah Narrative

Terry Stauffer

Introduction

Right theology matters very much because God matters very much. The story of Elijah in First Kings is compelling, but what are we looking for when we read? The greatest benefit of studying God's Word is absorbing what it tells us about God so that we might worship and live in ways that please him.

The ministry of Elijah marks a new era in the history of God's people, the beginning of the age of the prophets. In Elijah's story, we see many signs of power. As we read, we should remember that almost all of the miracles in the Bible are found in the Exodus account, the Elijah/Elisha narrative and in the record of Christ and the apostles at the birth of the church. It is not a coincidence that these signs accompany a new season of revelation. In First Kings, these miracles reveal the authority of the prophet Elijah and, subsequently, the authority of the prophets that follow him. The miracles of Elijah and his corresponding words of authority come down to us in God's inerrant Word. God's Word to his idolatrous people in Elijah's day is his Word to us today.

God is the Living God

One of the basic but essential theological lessons from this part of biblical history is that God is alive, active and involved in his world. This God is not a human-like god or a force, let alone a mere tradition or human projection.

We must not let our interest in the history of the Bible or even our theological pursuits dull us to the reality that God is living and active in the world. We are his creatures. He is our creator and owner.

God Speaks

God called all that has been made into being by the power of his Word. We have a written record of God's words in the Scriptures. God spoke many times through Elijah and he spoke directly to Elijah in words of comfort and instruction. God is and God speaks.

God is Sovereign Over Nature

Elijah told King Ahab that there would not be rain in Israel for a few years.[28] God's presence and power were made known to Ahab and the people through this terrible drought and the famine that came with it.[29]

God provided for Elijah during the beginning of this famine through the agency of ravens. God then sent him to Sidon, to the home of a

---

[28] Virtually any commentary will point out that Baal was considered the storm god. Even without this background information, it is obvious that this drought was a judgment upon the misplaced worship of Ahab and his people.

[29] Note that First Kings does not give us a specific number of years, but both James and Jesus (Jas. 5:17; Luke 4:25) say time of the famine was 3 ½ years long (compare also Rev. 11:6). We read about the miraculous end of the drought in 18:41-46.

CHAPTER 7: The Doctrine of God in the Elijah Narrative

widow. God fed that household miraculously until the famine ended. These were both signs of God's sovereignty over nature.

While Elijah was in Zarephath, the widow's son died. God raised this boy from the dead through the prophet's intercession. God is sovereign over all of nature, even over the greatest enemy, death. Note the widow's confession in 17:24: "Now I know that you are a man of God, and that the word of the LORD in your mouth is truth."

God is Sovereign Over Other Nations

The Elijah narrative makes it clear that God is not a local deity. God is not limited in power outside of his own territory—the whole earth is his possession.

The main event in Elijah's career is his showdown with the prophets of Baal (1 Ki. 18:1-40). The one true God is God alone. The other gods are nothing. Note Elijah's simple prayer in 18:36-37. God answered that prayer immediately and dramatically with consuming fire from heaven. As for the false prophets' desperate pleadings, see 18:29—"there was no voice. No one answered; no one paid attention."

Later in the account, Israel went to war against the Syrians (20:13-30). Even though they were greatly outnumbered, the LORD gave the victory to Ahab and his army. The Syrians reasoned that the God of Israel must be a god of the hills, not a god of the plains. So, they fought again on the plain and were defeated again. In 20:28 God says that the battle was given to Israel so that they would "know that I am the LORD."

Through the prophets, God spoke to the nations as well as Israel and Judah. He even called future kings by name and predicted particular judgments. We must not forget that no matter how chaotic our world seems, God is still sovereign over the nations.

God is Jealous for His Glory

The showdown on Mount Carmel was not just to show that God was better than Baal. God alone demands worship and submission from his creatures. A blending of true worship with other religions is not acceptable. "How long will you go limping between two opinions?" Elijah asked the people in 18:21.

When God revealed his power before the people, they cried out, "The LORD, he is God; the LORD, he is God" (18:39). Jezebel was not impressed. She responded by threatening to kill Elijah. She did not fear the LORD. Neither did King Ahab. There was no reform movement initiated by the people, either. They quietly followed their wicked leaders, even after Mount Carmel.

Ahab stood in a long line of wicked kings of Israel who distorted the worship of God. His predecessor Jeroboam introduced the worship of golden calves in Israel (1 Ki. 12:26-33). These calves were supposed to represent the one true God, but this commandment-breaking worship was wicked. He, and all of Israel, should have remembered the worship of the golden calf in the wilderness (Exodus 32). From this time on, the kings of the northern kingdom of Israel were judged by the wicked standard of the innovator, Jeroboam.[30]

The Lord hates all false worship. It lies about him and it hurts people as it brings upon them the curses of the covenant (see Deut. 28). One of the clear applications for us is that we must worship God alone and not, as Elijah put it, be "limping between two opinions" (18:21).

God is Patient and Merciful With His People

When Ahab built a temple to Baal in Samaria, fire should have come down from heaven to destroy it. We who read this history might think that God would have been entirely just in sending Israel into captivity in

---

[30] See, for example, 16:19, 26 regarding Zimri and Omri, respectively.

CHAPTER 7: The Doctrine of God in the Elijah Narrative

930 BC instead of postponing judgment until 721 BC. But not only did God show great patience to the kings of Israel, he also gave them warnings and signs through the prophets. King Ahab was given many opportunities to recognize the one true God and obey him, but he persisted in evil.

Mercifully, God allows people to question him. In 17:17-24, the grief-stricken Sidonian widow complained to Elijah about God's purposes for her and her household. At this point, even Elijah questioned God, but God did not get angry. He heard these confused cries and responded with a compassionate miracle.

When Elijah fled from Jezebel, God provided for his physical needs. He worked Elijah's flight into an important lesson for him and for us. We learn of God's providence and guidance. We are reminded of Moses at Mount Horeb (Ex. 3; Ex. 33-34), and we see that Elijah was a man like us (Jas. 5:17). This is all for our instruction and encouragement, but it is also a reminder of God's kindness and patience.

God is the Righteous Judge

While God is patient and compassionate, he is also just. In the Elijah narrative, we see several examples that shout out to us that sin has consequences. These are not merely natural consequences, but active judgments of God.

Even in the first chapter of the Elijah narrative (1 Ki. 17), the drought is brought on as judgment upon Israel and her neighbors for their refusal to worship God on his terms. The famine caused by the drought would have brought widespread hardship. The widow's report that she was preparing to die is an indication that the famine must have been severe.

Both the word of the prophet and the exile of Elijah are evidences of judgment upon a stubborn people and their rebellious king. Jesus made a theological application of this reality in Luke 4:25-26:

But in truth, I tell you, there were many widows in Israel in the days of Elijah, when the heavens were shut up three years and six months, and a great famine came over all the land, and Elijah was sent to none of them but only to Zarephath, in the land of Sidon, to a woman who was a widow.

When Jesus made this point, the people in his hometown were "filled with wrath," and even tried to kill him. People by nature hate God's truth, but God will judge those who reject his prophets. Even more seriously, God will judge those who reject his Son.

In chapter 18, 450 prophets of Baal were slaughtered. This was brutal, but necessary. These zealous false prophets were leading the people of Israel to break covenant with their Lord and Redeemer.

God destroys the kings and armies of other nations (20:13-34, for instance). We are not to read these victories in First Kings as God's reward for Israel's faithfulness. They were not following God's ways at this time. God used even a disobedient people to carry out his judgment upon other nations.

For a more personal instance of God's judgment, consider the grisly consequences for Ahab and Jezebel because of their murder of Naboth. Elijah announced that the kingdom would be taken from their line and that the dogs would lick up Ahab's blood and consume Jezebel (21:17-24). These things did come to pass, just as Elijah had said (22:37, 38; 2 Ki. 9:30-37).

In chapter 22, Micaiah's prophecy pulls back the curtain on the heavenly throne room. The Lord intended to send Ahab to death in battle. One of the messengers before God's throne offers to be a "lying spirit" in the mouths of the prophets to ensure this outcome. In the passage, 400 prophets have urged Ahab on to victory. Micaiah was the only one who told the truth to Ahab.

When we examine this scene in context, we see that Ahab, predictably, rejected the true prophet's warning and even had him punished. The LORD's righteous judgment upon Ahab came in the

CHAPTER 7: The Doctrine of God in the Elijah Narrative

form of the lying prophets and his death in battle. Ahab willingly suppressed the truth and refused to worship God according to his Word. He led the people into idolatry and could not escape God's just judgment.

These are just a few of the many theological lessons that we learn from the Elijah narrative in First Kings. But before we conclude, we should consider some links to the New Testament as we read this Old Testament history.

Links to the New Testament

Elijah was anticipated as the forerunner to the Messiah (Mal. 4:5). Jesus affirmed this fulfillment in the person of John the Baptist (see, for instance, Matt. 11:14, 17:11). The greatness and uniqueness of Christ stands out in relief as we compare him to both Elijah and John the Baptist.

Food miracles are a part of the Elijah story, and these may remind us of Jesus turning water to wine (Jn. 2), or the feeding of the five thousand (Matt. 14). We read in Luke 7 that Jesus raised a widow's son, an account that has several parallels with Elijah's raising of the widow's son in First Kings 17. When we compare these miracles, Jesus again shines in glory. His miracles originated in him as the creator. He is no mere prophet, he is Lord.

No theological study of the Elijah narrative would be complete without a mention of Elijah's ascension to heaven, accompanied by chariots of fire (2 Ki. 2:11-12).[31] Only Elijah and Enoch escaped death in this way (Gen. 5:24, compare Heb. 11:5). There was, however, another one who ascended to heaven—the only one to do so in a resurrected, everlasting body. Elijah was a sinful man in need of a redeemer, but as the premier Old Testament prophet, he pointed to

---

[31] The scope of this brief study corresponds to the fall 2015 Calvary Grace Church preaching series on First Kings, but I trust that moving into Second Kings to make this point is useful.

Christ, the sinless Messiah.[32] Elijah's ascension was a foreshadowing of the ascension of our Lord after his death and resurrection.

Be freshly amazed at God's power in the miracles that attended Elijah's ministry, but let your thoughts and your worship be drawn to the greater Prophet, Priest and King, the God-Man, our Lord Jesus Christ.

---

[32] Consider, too, how he appeared with Moses to confer with Jesus on the Mount of Transfiguration (Matthew 17).

APPENDIX A

Chronologies of Rulers, Prophets, and Events in the Book of Kings

Jeff Jones

1. Chronology of the Rulers of Judah

Name	Regnal Dates (BC)	Scripture Passages	Theological Evaluation
Rehoboam	931/930 - 915/914	1 Kings 12:1-24, 1 Kings 14:21-31, 2 Chronicles 10-12	Evil
Abijam	915/914 - 912/911	1 Kings 15:1-8, 2 Chronicles 11:22, 13:1-22	Evil
Asa	912/911 - 871-870	1 Kings 15:9-24, 2 Chronicles 14-16	Mostly Good
Jehoshaphat	871/870 - 848/847 (co-regency 871)	1 Kings 22:1-50, 2 Chronicles 17-20	Mostly Good
J(eh)oram I	848/847 - 842 (co-regency 853)	2 Kings 8:16-24, 2 Chronicles 21	Evil
Ahaziah II	842 - 841	2 Kings 8:25-29, 9:14-29, 2 Chronicles 22:1-9	Evil
Athaliah (regent for Joash)	841 - 835	2 Kings 11:1-20, 2 Chronicles 22:10-12, 23:1-15	Extremely Evil
J(eh)oash I	841/835 - 797/796	2 Kings 11 - 12:21, 2 Chronicles 22:10 - 24:27	Mostly Good

Chronology of the Rulers of Judah (cont'd)

Name	Regnal Dates (BC)	Scripture Passages	Theological Evaluation
Amaziah	797/796 - 768/767	2 Kings 14:1-22, 2 Chronicles 25	Mostly Good
Azariah (Uzziah)	767/766 - 736/735 (co-regency 787ff., not active due to disease 750ff.)	2 Kings 15:1-7, 2 Chronicles 26	Mostly Good
J(eh)otham	752/751 - 732/731	2 Kings 15:32-38, 2 Chronicles 27	Mostly Good
Ahaz	732/731 - 716 (co-regency 736/735ff.)	2 Kings 16:1-20, 2 Chronicles 28:1-27	Evil
Hezekiah	716 - 687/686 (co-regency 729ff.)	2 Chronicles 29-32, 2 Kings 18-20	Very Good
Manasseh	687/686 - 643 (co-regency 698/697ff.)	2 Kings 21:1-18, 2 Chronicles 33:1-20	Extremely Evil
Amon	643 - 641	2 Kings 21:19-26, 2 Chronicles 33:21-25	Extremely Evil
Josiah	641 - 609	2 Kings 22-23:30, 2 Chronicles 34-35	Very Good
Jehoahaz II	609 (three months)	2 Kings 23:31-34, 2 Chronicles 36:1-4	Evil
Jehoiakim	609-598	2 Kings 23:35-24:7, 2 Chronicles 36:5-8, Jeremiah 36	Evil
Jehoiachin	598/597 (three months)	2 Kings 24:8-17, 25:27-30, 2 Chronicles 36:9-10, Jeremiah 52:31-34	Evil
Zedekiah	597-586	2 Kings 24:18 - 25:7, 2 Chronicles 36:11-21, Jeremiah 32-34, 37-39:10, 52:1-30	Evil

APPENDIX A: Chronologies

2. Chronology of the Rulers of Israel

Name	Regnal Dates (BC)	Scripture Passages
Founding Dynasty of Jeroboam I		
Jeroboam I	922-901	1 Kings 11:26-40; 1 Kings 12:21-14:20
Nadab	901-900	1 Kings 15:25-32
Dynasty of Baasha		
Baasha	900-877	1 Kings 15:33-16:7
Elah	877-876	1 Kings 16:8-14
Military Coup		
Zimri	876	1 Kings 16:15-20
Dynasty of the Omrides		
Omri	876-869	1 Kings 16:21-28
Ahab	869-850	1 Kings 16:29-22:40
Ahaziah	850-849	1 Kings 22:51-2 Kings 1:18
J(eh)oram	849-842/841	2 Kings 3:1-9:29
Dynasty of Jehu		
Jehu	842/841-815	2 Kings 9:1-10:36
Jehoahaz	815-801	2 Kings 13:1-9
J(eh)oash	801-786	2 Kings 13:10-14:16

Chronology of the Rulers of Israel (cont'd)

Name	Regnal Dates (BC)	Scripture Passages
Dynasty of Jehu (continued)		
Jeroboam II	786-746	2 Kings 14:23-29
Zechariah	746-745	2 Kings 15:8-12
Last Kings of Northern Tribes		
Shallum	745	2 Kings 15:13-16
Menahem	745-737	2 Kings 15:17-22
Pekahiah	737-736	2 Kings 15:23-26
Pekah	736-732	2 Kings 15:27-31
Hoshea	732-724	2 Kings 17:1-6
Fall of Samaria	722/21	2 Kings 17:1-41

APPENDIX A: Chronologies

3. Chronology of Major Historical Events and Prophetic Ministries

Date	Biblical Event	Prophetic Ministry	Extrabiblical Events
960 BC	David's death		
	Solomon becomes king		
956 BC	Temple construction begins		
922 BC	Israel divided into northern & southern kingdoms		
853 BC			Battle of Qarqar
835 BC - 796 BC	Reign of Joash over northern kingdom	Joel's ministry (approximate, assuming early date)	
780 BC		Jonah's ministry (approximate - 2 Ki. 14:25)	
760 BC		Amos' ministry (approximate)	
753 BC	Death of Jeroboam II	Hosea's ministry begins (latest possible date, could have started earlier)	
740 BC	Azariah/Uzziah's death (Isaiah's vision in Is. 6)	Isaiah's ministry begins	

Chronology of Major Historical Events and Prophetic Ministries (cont'd)

Date	Biblical Event	Prophetic Ministry	Extrabiblical Events
735 BC		Micah's ministry begins (earliest possible date)	
722/721 BC	Samaria falls	Hosea's ministry ends (approximate)	
	Northern kingdom ends		
701 BC	Assyrians under Sennacherib invade Judah	Micah's ministry ends (approximate)	
687/686 BC	Hezekiah's death	Isaiah's ministry ends (earliest possible date, probably later)	
640 BC	Josiah becomes king	Zephaniah's ministry begins (earliest possible date)	
627 BC		Jeremiah's ministry begins (Jer. 1:2)	
615 BC		Nahum's ministry begins (possibly)	Medes and Persians form alliance
612 BC		Nahum's ministry ends	Babylon captures Nineveh

APPENDIX A: Chronologies

Chronology of Major Historical Events and Prophetic Ministries (cont'd)

Date	Biblical Event	Prophetic Ministry	Extrabiblical Events
609 BC	Battle of Megiddo	Zephaniah's ministry ends (latest possible date)	
	King Josiah dies		
608 BC - 606 BC		Habakkuk's ministry (approximate)	
605 BC	First Babylonian Deportation	Daniel's ministry begins	Battle of Carchemish - Babylon defeats Egypt
	Daniel & friends sent to Babylon		
597 BC (March 16)	Second Babylonian Deportation		
	King Jehoiachin & Ezekiel exiled		
593 BC		Ezekiel's ministry begins	
587/586 BC	Babylon destroys Jerusalem		
	Final Babylonian Deportation (King Zedekiah exiled)		

Chronology of Major Historical Events and Prophetic Ministries (cont'd)[33]

Date	Biblical Event	Prophetic Ministry	Extrabiblical Events
587/586 BC - 538 BC	Exile in Babylon		
585 BC	Judean remnant flees to Egypt with Jeremiah	Jeremiah's ministry ends (earliest possible date)	
585 BC - 580 BC		Obadiah's ministry (approximate)	
571 BC		Ezekiel's ministry ends	
560 BC	Jehoiachin granted mercy (Jer. 52:31-34)		Evil-Merodach succeeds Nebuchadnezzar
560 BC - 539 BC		Writing of Kings (approximate)	
539 BC	Persians conquer Babylon		
536 BC		End of Daniel's ministry (approximate)	
538 BC	Edict of Cyrus allowing Jews to return		

[33] These three chronologies originated as an assignment I was given in an Old Testament class at Canadian Southern Baptist Seminary, and were compiled from information found in the following sources: Jack Finegan, *Handbook of Biblical Chronology*, rev. ed. (Peabody: Hendrickson, 1998); K.M. Heim, "Kings and Kingship," in *Dictionary of the Old Testament Historical Books*, ed. Bill Arnold and H.G.M. Williamson, pp. 610-623 (Downers Grove: InterVarsity, 2005); K.A. Kitchen, "Chronology," in *Dictionary of the Old Testament Historical Books*, ed. Bill Arnold and H.G.M. Williamson, pp. 181-188 (Downers Grove: InterVarsity, 2005); Thomas Brisco, *The Holman Bible Atlas* (Nashville: Broadman & Holman, 1998).

APPENDIX B

Further Reading

1. Commentaries

Paul R. House. *1, 2 Kings*, **New American Commentary. Nashville: Broadman & Holman, 1995.**

House's excellent commentary was key to the study that produced our fall 2015 preaching series and this book of essays on First Kings. If someone only has one volume on Kings, this should be the one. This commentary is conservative and evangelical.

Mark Dever. "The Message of 1 Kings: Decline," in *The Message of the Old Testament: Promises Made.* **Wheaton: Crossway, 2006.**

Very accessible and approachable, Dever's article on First Kings was originally a sermon—preached as an overview of the book at Capitol Hill Baptist Church. As such, it provides a great place to start devotional study of First Kings and useful ideas for teaching and preaching. This article and the entire volume containing it is conservative and evangelical.

Dale Ralph Davis. *1 Kings: The Wisdom and the Folly*, **Focus on the Bible. Fearn: Christian Focus, 2007.**

This commentary is accessible and very useful for scholars, pastors, and Bible study leaders alike. It is less technical and more expositional, providing thought-provoking illustrations and applications with a strong pastoral tone. This commentary is conservative and evangelical.

Peter J. Leithart. *1 & 2 Kings*, **Brazos Theological Commentary. Grand Rapids: Baker, 2006.**

While not as technical or detailed as House, Leithart does an excellent job placing Kings in its redemptive-historical context and tracing theological themes in the work. His introductory article on "1-2 Kings as Gospel" is almost worth the price of the book alone. This commentary is conservative and evangelical, though the reader is cautioned that Leithart writes from a more sacramental and ecumenical perspective than we could ourselves comfortably affirm.

Richard D. Patterson. "1 & 2 Kings," in *1 & 2 Kings, 1 & 2 Chronicles, Ezra, Nehemiah, Esther, Job*, **Expositor's Bible Commentary. Grand Rapids: Zondervan, 1988.**

Patterson's commentary, though somewhat older, remains good. It is useful for its treatment of higher criticism. This commentary is conservative and evangelical.

Matthew Henry. "An Exposition, With Practical Observations, On The First Book Of Kings," in *Commentary on the Whole Bible*, **Volume II. www.ccel.org/ccel/henry/mhc2.iKi.i.html**

As useful as recent historical discoveries and academic discussion may be, the insights of pastors like Matthew Henry remain perennial for any student of the Bible.

2. Theology

Graeme Goldsworthy. *Christ-Centered Biblical Theology: Hermeneutical Foundations and Principles.* **Downers Grove: Intervarsity Press, 2012.**

Any of Goldsworthy's works are useful, and this is no exception. In this work, he argues that some of the classical foci of Reformed theology, such as Moses and the Decalogue, are not actually where the major emphasis of the New Testament is—namely, and relevant for a study of Kings, David and the Son of David. His section on the David & Solomon axis in redemptive history is extremely helpful.

Thomas Schreiner. *The King In His Beauty: A Biblical Theology of the Old and New Testaments.* **Grand Rapids: Baker Academic, 2013.**

Another very helpful big-picture overview of how God has unfolded his plan of salvation through history, useful for locating themes like wisdom in the context of the entire Bible.

G.K. Beale. *The Temple and the Church's Mission: A Biblical Theology of the Dwelling Place of God.* **Downers Grove: IVP Academic, 2004.**

Beale's examination of the redemptive-historical development of the theme of God's dwelling place is very helpful for anyone trying to understand the Temple narrative in the book of First Kings.

3. Devotional

Thomas Watson. *The Godly Man's Picture.* **Carlisle: Banner of Truth Trust, 1992.**

This Puritan classic, originally written in 1666, aims to draw "with a Scripture Pencil...Some Characteristic Marks of a Man who is Going to Heaven." For the modern-day Christian seeking wisdom, Watson remains as relevant as when he first wrote.

Index

Abijah, 40
abomination, 16
Absalom, 20-22, 24
Acts of Solomon (book), 4
Adam, 17, 34
Adonijah, 15, 19-22, 24
Ahab, 5, 7, 46-48, 50, 55
Ahijah, 34
altar, 32, 37-39
Amaziah, 38, 54
Amnon, 20-22, 24
anger, 21
annals, 3
ark, 5, 14
Asa, 38, 53
ascension, 51-52
Assyria, 4, 7, 17, 58
Athaliah, 7, 53
authority, 21, 34, 45
Azariah (Uzziah), 38, 54, 57

Baal, 46-48, 50
Babylon, 2-4, 6, 17, 58-60
Barzillai, sons of, 23
Bathsheba, 15, 19, 22
bronze, 12, 26,
Buddhism, 41

calf/calves, 37, 40, 48
Canaan, 33
captivity, 48
Carmel, Mount, 47-48
Cave of Adullam, 13
character, 22-23
characterization, 7-8

Chemosh, 32
children, 19-24
Christos, 17
Chronicles, 1st, 4-5
Chronicles, 2nd, 3-5
Chronicles of the Kings of Israel, 4-5
Chronicles of the Kings of Judah, 4
chronicles (general), 3
church, xii, 42-43, 45
compromise, 32, 35, 37
covenant, 8-9, 13, 32, 48, 50
Cyrus, 3, 6, 60

Daniel, 6, 59-60
David, xi-xiii, 3, 7, 12-18, 19-24, 31, 34-35, 37-38, 57, 63
destruction, 7, 41
Deuteronomy, 7-8, 40-41
discipline, 19-23
disobedience, 12, 31-33, 35
doctrine, 22, 45
dynastic/dynasty, 16, 55-56

Egypt, 12, 32, 40, 59-60
Egyptian, 4, 12
Eli, 20
Elijah, 7-8, 34, 45-52
Elisha, 8, 34, 45
empire, 11-12
Enoch, 51
Eve, 34
evil, 7, 20, 38, 49, 53-54
Evil-Merodach, 3, 60
exile, xii, 1-4, 6, 17, 34, 49, 59-60
exilic, 4

Exodus, 13, 40, 45
Ezekiel, 6, 34, 59-60

false, 8, 31-32, 47-48, 50
famine, 46, 49
fatherhood, 19, 24
femininity, 23
folly, 21, 31-32
food, xiii, 51
fool/foolish, xi, 14, 19

genre, 6-8
glory, vii, xi-xii, 7, 9, 29, 41, 47, 51
godliness, 26-27
gold, 12, 16, 32, 37, 40, 48
golden age/years, xi, 11-12, 16
Goliath, 12-13, 15

Hezekiah, 7, 38, 54, 58
high places, 35, 37-42
Hinduism, 41
hinge, 11, 14-16
Hiram of Tyre, 26
history, xi-xii, 2, 4-9, 11, 14-15, 17, 34, 45-46, 48, 51, 63
historical, xi, 5, 7-8, 16, 57-60, 62
Holy Spirit, 2, 41
Horeb, Mount, 49
house, 14, 17-18, 39-40
household, 46, 49
hymn, 42
hypocrite, 22

idolatry, 32, 34, 37, 39, 51
inerrancy/inerrant, 5, 45
instruction, 22-23, 32-33, 46, 49
integrity, 5, 22
intermarriage, 16
Islam, 41

James, 26, 46
Jehoash, 38, 53, 55
Jehoiachin, 2-3, 6-7, 54, 59-60
Jehoiakim, 6, 54
Jeremiah, 1-2, 34, 58, 60
Jeroboam, 7, 37, 39-40, 48, 55-57
Jerusalem, 3, 4, 7, 13-14, 17-18, 39-41, 59
Jezebel, 7, 48-50
Joab, 19, 23
John the Baptist, 13, 51
Jonathan, 13, 16
Joshua (book), 1-3, 8
Joshua (leader), xi, 2
Josiah, 7, 38, 54, 58-59
Jotham, 38
Judah, 3-4, 6, 17, 38, 47, 53-54, 58
Judges (book), 1-3, 41
judges (rulers), 12
judgment, 3, 33-34, 38, 46-47, 49-51

knowledge, 25-26, 28

land, 2, 33, 40, 49-50
Law of Moses, 8, 23, 32-33
leader, 31, 48
leadership, 23-24, 34
Levitical, 37-38
libraries, 3
Lord's Day, 42
Lord's Supper, 42

Manasseh, 7, 38, 54
marriage, 32
masculinity, 23
Messiah, xiii, 52
Micaiah, 50
military, 3, 13, 15-16, 55
miracle, 45, 49, 51-52
Moabite, 16

Index

Molech, 32
monarchy, xi, 15, 17
Moses, 2, 8, 14, 32, 49-50, 63

Naboth, 40
narrative, xii, 6-8, 45, 47, 49, 51, 63
nation/nations, xii, 4, 8, 12-13, 16-17, 34, 39, 47, 50
nature, 12, 26, 46-47, 50
New Covenant, 24, 41
New Testament, 17, 23, 42-43, 51, 63
north/northern, 3-4, 7, 12, 37, 48, 56-57

obedience, 25, 29, 32, 34-35, 39
Old Covenant, 42
Old Testament, xii, 15, 17, 35, 41, 51
Omri, 5, 48, 55

pagan, 39-40, 42
Paul (apostle), 23, 42
Pax Americana, 11
Pax Britannica, 11
Pax Christi, 18
Pax Davidica, 14
Pax Romana, 11
Pax Solomonica, 11-12, 16-18
peace, 11-12, 14, 16, 18, 34-35
Pentateuch, 2
Persia, 6, 58, 60
Pharaoh, 12, 16-17
Philistine, 12-13
piety, xiii, 13, 15, 32
Pisgah, 14
platform, 40
plot, 6-8
post-exilic, 4
prayer/prayerful, 16, 42, 47
preaching, 28, 42, 61
priest, 37, 40, 47, 52

priesthood, 37
promise, xiii, 2-3, 7-8, 12, 14, 19, 24, 29, 33-35, 39
Promised Land, 2, 12, 14, 16
prophecy, 17, 50
prophet/prophetic, xi, 6-9, 17, 34, 45, 47-52, 57-60
prophetic narrative, 8
prophetic-historical narrative, 8
proverbs, 21-22, 26, 28
providence, 4, 49

Queen of Sheba, 17

redeemer, 50-51
regent, 14, 53
Rehoboam, 12, 38, 53
rest, 14, 33
restoration, 7
ruler, 13, 17, 53-56

Samaria, 4, 7, 48, 56
Samaritan, 41
Samuel (books), 1-3, 14, 20
Samuel (prophet), 2, 12
Satan, 35
Saul (king), 12-13, 16
Saul of Tarsus, 18
security, 27, 40
shepherd, xiii, 12
Shimei, 23
Sidon/Sidonian, 16, 46, 49-50
sin, xii-xiii, 20-22, 24, 29, 31, 34-35, 49, 51
Sinai, 40
slavery, 12
son, xi, xiii, 14-15, 19-23, 32, 37-38, 40, 42, 47, 50-51
Son of David, xiii, 14, 16-18, 24, 34, 63
song, 13, 42

sovereign/sovereignty, 27, 33-34, 46-47
source, xii, 2-5, 7, 27
south, 12, 57
Syria/Syrian, 47

Tamar, 20
teaching, 23, 28, 43, 61
temple, xii, 12, 14, 16, 18, 26, 33, 35, 37-41, 48, 57, 63
theocracy, xii
theology, 45, 62-63
trade, 32
training, 20-21
treaties, 3, 16

understanding, 2, 25-28
Uriah, 22

Uzziah (Azariah), 38, 54, 57

wealth, 16, 31-35
widow, 46-47, 49-51
wilderness, 41, 48
wisdom, 15, 17, 25-29, 31-32, 35, 63
wives, 16, 29, 31-33
women, 16, 22, 29, 32
Word, 28, 32-35, 42, 45-47, 51
worship, 16-17, 31-33, 37-42, 45-50, 52

Zarephath, 47, 50
Zimri, 5, 48, 55
Zion, 11, 13-14, 41

About the Authors

Clint Humfrey

Clint was born and raised on a farm south of Calgary. Clint was converted to Christ as an adult. Soon after he pursued training in theology. He has taken diploma studies at The Master's College in California, and completed his Bachelor of Ministry at Prairie Bible College and Master of Divinity at Toronto Baptist Seminary. Clint previously served as pastor at a church in Blackie, Alberta. Afterward for three years he taught New Testament Greek as a professor at Toronto Baptist Seminary. Clint was the founding pastor and church planter of Calvary Grace Church in November 2006. He and his wife Christel live in High River, Alberta with their three children.

Paul Toews

Paul was born in Winnipeg, Manitoba. He put his trust in Christ at the age of 12 and at age 18 he moved to Calgary. He attended the University of Calgary where he received a Bachelor of Arts in Psychology with a minor in Sociology. He then went to the University of Alberta where he earned a Bachelor of Education. Paul is a schoolteacher with experience teaching elementary school students and presently teaches at a middle school in northwest Calgary while pursuing a Master of Science degree in Educational Leadership. Paul lives in Calgary with his wife Melody, their four daughters, and some tarantulas.

Terry Stauffer

Terry was born and raised in northern Alberta but spent 14 years in

British Columbia, including study at Northwest Baptist Theological College and the ACTS Seminary at Trinity Western University. Terry was raised in a Christian home and trusted Christ at an early age. He pastored churches in Barriere, B.C. (1990-1995) and Edson, Alberta (1997-2011) before coming to Calvary Grace. Terry moved to Calgary with his wife, Juanita and two daughters in October, 2011. Terry and Juanita also have another daughter who preceded them to Heaven in 2008 and a grown son who is married and living in Eastern Canada.

Gavin Peacock

Gavin was born in Kent, England, where he played professional soccer for 18 years. He was converted to Christ at age 18 and was used by God to bear witness to the gospel throughout his career. In 2006 God called him to pastoral ministry, and after moving to Calgary in 2008, he graduated from seminary with a Master of Arts in Christian Studies. In February 2012 Calvary Grace commissioned him as Home Missionary. He now serves full-time as a Pastor at Calvary Grace Church, and is Director of International Outreach for the Council for Biblical Manhood and Womanhood. Gavin lives in Canmore, Alberta with his wife, Amanda, and they have two grown children.

Jeff Jones

Jeff was born in British Columbia to a Christian family. He joined the Canadian Army at 17, earning a Bachelor of Arts in Business Administration, with a minor in Military Psychology and Leadership, from the Royal Military College. In 2003, God used a training injury to awaken Jeff to living faith in Christ. Leaving the Army in 2005 he took a Master of Divinity from Canadian Southern Baptist Seminary in Cochrane, Alberta. Jeff pastored at a Southern Baptist church in Calgary (2006-2008) before Calvary Grace, and also is a corporate chaplain. He and his wife Erin live in Cochrane with their six children.

About Calvary Grace Church

Calvary Grace Church is an evangelical partnership of believers in Jesus Christ committed to seeing God glorified in the area of Calgary, Alberta, Canada and beyond.

We are gathered around the expository preaching of God's Word and hold to the theology of the Protestant Reformation, striving to become more like Christ and to proclaim the Good News of his Kingdom in gratitude to the God who saved us by his sovereign grace.

For more information, please visit our website at:

www.calvarygrace.ca

www.ingramcontent.com/pod-product-compliance
Lightning Source LLC
Chambersburg PA
CBHW031415040426

42444CB00005B/574